UNSHAKABLE FAITH

By
Dr. Benjamin Hinton, D.Min.

2509 Saddlehorse Lane
Gastonia, NC 28056
Tabernacle Baptist Church
704. 864. 4051

Chosen Word Publishing
Charlotte, North Carolina

Unshakable Faith Copyright ©1999
by Dr. Benjamin Hinton,D.Min.

Scriptures taken from King James Version, New King James Version and the New International Version of the Bible.

ISBN 0974805653

Published by Chosen Word Publishing, Charlotte, N.C.
www.chosenwordpublishing.com

You may contact Dr. Benjamin Hinton at:
www.eteamministry.org
hinton@chosenwordpublishing.com

Preface

This book is a facilitator, rather than a substitute for extensive study of the Christian Faith and New Testament Theology. It is designed to be a user-friendly study manual for personal, group, or other class study. It serves as an introduction to our Christian Doctrine. The focus of this work is to highlight some of the key biblical, theological, and doctrinal truths that we embrace as part of our Christian faith.

It is impossible to cover such an extensive volume of literature in a short time or even in one book. My purpose here is simply to provide an introduction in order to inspire further study. This book is designed with scholastic depth; it is user friendly for both pastors and laity. I pray that each reader's appreciation for the Word of God will equip you for qualitative Christian living and service. I pray also that you will go forth and share your knowledge with others as you *"rightly divide the word of truth"* in your perspective ministries. We are called to be doers of the Word and not hearers only (Matthew 7:24-27; James 1:22-25). May you be blessed as you continue your theological quest in Kingdom living with an unshakable faith.

Dr. Benjamin Hinton, D. Min.
Gastonia, North Carolina

Dedication

This book is dedicated to a host of very special people in my life who are a constant source of strength and support. First, I give the highest glory to our Heavenly Father, to Jesus Christ our Lord, and to the Holy Spirit.

To my wonderful wife Tangela, you are my true confidant, cheerleader, friend, prayer partner and partner in marriage and ministry. I dedicate this work to my two sons of thunder Benjamin Samuel and Nathaniel Robert who share Daddy with the world.

I am grateful for my wonderful parents, Deacon Robert Hinton, Sr. and Mrs. Natha Hinton of Hamilton, Georgia. You are the ones that birthed me, nurtured me, and introduced me to God and His Word. I give my special thanks to my parents by marriage, Deacon Samuel and Gwendolyn White of Macon, Georgia. I'm grateful to my seven siblings who have always been a constant support. To all the wonderful members of the Tabernacle Baptist Church in Gastonia, North Carolina where I've been privileged to serve as Pastor-Teacher. I am grateful to my pastoral friends and colleagues across denominational lines, too many to list.

Finally to all of my faculty colleagues and students of the Jernigan Theological Studies-Advanced Projects Division of the National Baptist Congress of Christian Education, an auxiliary of the National Baptist Convention, U.S.A., Inc. This book was initially developed as a teaching manual for the class I have taught for several years, Introduction to New Testament Theology. A very special thanks to my colleagues in that division, particularly Dr. Elliot Cuff, Ms. Dorothy Montgomery, Dr. Robert Scott, Dr. Robert Baynum, Dr. George W. Waddles Sr. (Dean), Dr. R.B. Holmes Jr. (President). Special thanks to Mrs. Jeannette T. Gregory, Sara Dobie and the staff of Chosen Word Publishing for their professional expertise in the publication of this book.

CONTENTS

INTRODUCTION

The Bible is **THE BOOK** of the Christian Faith. It is the living Word that guides our lives as the foundation of our faith. It is the written record of the divine revelation of God to us and for us. We live in a time where there is a growing sense of doctrinal and theological confusion concerning our common faith in Christ. There are many factors that divide Christian believers in the body of Christ. While many may be divided in our denominational preferences, our preaching and teaching styles, our modes of baptism, and our styles of worship may vary. However, the central factor that unites us together is the universal faith in the Bible (the Word of God) and our resurrected Savior Jesus Christ.

Our mutual faith unites us across racial, social, ethnic, cultural, and denominational grounds. Our faith has been the key to our strength, survival, sanity, and success in a sinful world. We can and must respect all the above-mentioned differences, and come to a concerted agreement with the Apostle Paul who exhorts us, ***"Make every effort to keep the unity of the Spirit in the bond of peace. There is one body and one Spirit, just as you were called, One Lord, one faith, one baptism; one God and Father of all, who is over all and through all and in all" (Ephesians 4:3-6, NIV).***

Many of the factors that divide us are doctrinal differences and man-made issues rather than God ordained differences. Over the centuries, much has been added to the Word from the philosophies and doctrinal ideologies of man and, as a result, many people are confused about what is biblically sound doctrine. There is a paradigm shift in the body of Christ. Some churches are experiencing tremendous growth, while others are either holding on or simply striving to survive. There are others that are declining. With the emergence of so many Churches, Temples, Worship Centers, and Ministries, many believers get lost in the shuffle of doctrinal or theological confusion.

Then, there are other denominational groups that have been warring against one another for years over doctrinal issues such as the day of worship. Is it Saturday or Sunday? Other issues that divide us are the mode or method of baptism, and the baptismal formula. There are those who refer to themselves as the "Jesus only believers." They argue that we are baptized only *"in the name of Jesus"* according to Acts 2:38: ***"Then Peter said unto them, Repent, and be baptized every one of you in the name of Jesus Christ."*** There are others, this author included, who teach that we are to follow the baptismal formula set forth by Jesus in Mathew 28:20 which teach that we are to ***"baptize them in the name of the Father, and of the Son, and of the Holy Spirit."***

Then there are other differential issues regarding women in ministry, i.e. women pastors or deacons. Did God call a woman to preach?

There are those hard-core traditionally minded saints who put God in a church box and try to tell God who He can or cannot call. We must understand that God does what He wants to do and how He wants to do it without our vote. If we truly understand the infinity of God, we would know that it is God's prerogative to use willing vessels for his glory. None of these issues should be a hindrance to our growing faith. All of these can become carnal issues that divide the body of Christ in ways similar to the Corinthian problems Paul addressed in I Corinthians 3. The believers were arguing over petty issues that had no relevance to faith, spiritual growth, and development or advancement of the Kingdom of God.

Our focus should always be on how we can develop an unshakable faith that will enable us to live as abundant victorious citizens of the Kingdom of God and how to further carry out our Kingdom assignment through daily evangelism in the world (Matthew 28:19-20; Mark 16:15-16). We need to know in what we believe and in whom we believe as it relates to our personal relationship with Jesus Christ. We need to know the centrality of our Christian faith and worship. Many people worship many things that they deify as gods.

As true believers in Christ with an unshakable faith, we must develop the burden that Paul had for people to know and understand the truth of the Word:

"Brethren my hearts desire and prayer for Israel is, that they might be saved. For I bear them record that they have zeal of God, but not according to knowledge. For they being ignorant of God's righteousness, and going about to establish their own righteousness, have not submitted themselves unto the righteousness of God. For Christ is the end of the law for righteousness to everyone that believeth" (Romans 10:1-4).

As New Testament Christian believers we must be clear in our faith convictions about our devotion and worship to the true God. Jesus said to the woman at the well, *"But the hour cometh, and now is, when the true worshippers shall worship the Father in spirit and in truth; for the Father seeketh such to worship him. God is a Spirit: and they that worship Him must worship him in Spirit and in truth"* (John 4:23-24).

The Bible helps us to establish and affirm our Faith in God. Thus the starting point for the study of the Christian faith is the Bible (Old and New Testament), the written record of God's words and acts in history. Although the Bible is comprised of sixty-six books, it is really one book—one continuous story—with two distinct testaments. The term "testament" comes from the Latin word **testamentum**, meaning *"covenant"* or *"agreement."*

The Old Testament contains the covenant between God and the people of Israel. It tells of God's revelation and intervention in the life of His covenant people. The Old Testament lays the foundation for the New Testament. The foundation of our faith is established in the Old Testament and it is affirmed in the New Testament through the revelation of Jesus Christ. The New Covenant contains the covenant of grace between God and all humankind, which was prophesied in the Old Testament. The prophet Jeremiah prophesied of a new day in which God would establish a new covenant:

"Behold the days come, saith the LORD, that I will make a new covenant with the house of Israel, and with the house of Judah:
Not according to the covenant that I made with their fathers in the day that I took them by the hand to bring them out of the land of Egypt; which my covenant they break, although I was an husband unto them, saith the LORD:
But this shall be the covenant that I will make with the house of Israel: After those days, says the LORD, I will put my law in their inward parts, and write it in their hearts; and will be their God, and they shall be my people" (Jeremiah 31:31-33).

The foundation of our Christian faith is built upon the affirmations found in the Old and New Testament. It is our duty and responsibility to continue to build upon this unshakable foundation in order that we might establish a Christ-Centered, Bible-Based, and Holy Spirit-Led lifestyle that gives glory to our God. Jesus asked his disciples one day, **"Who do you say that I am?"** Peter responded, **"Thou art the**

Christ, the Son of the living God." Jesus then affirmed, *"Upon this rock I will build my church; and the gates of hell shall not prevail against it."*

We are a part of Christ's universal Church—not the Roman Catholic Church, but the Redemptive Church of Jesus Christ our lord. Christ has redeemed us from the curse of the law and sin through his precious blood. The apostle Paul further helps us to understand our redemptive position in Christ and our New Testament faith:

"Wherefore remember, that ye being times past Gentiles in the flesh...
That at that time ye were without Christ, being aliens from the commonwealth of Israel, and strangers from the covenants of promise, having no hope, and without God in the world:
But now in Christ Jesus ye who were far off are made nigh by the blood of Christ.
For through him we both have access by one Spirit unto the Father.
Now therefore ye are no more strangers and foreigners, but fellow citizens with the saints of the household of God.
And are built upon the foundation of the apostles and prophets, Jesus Christ himself being the chief corner stone." (Ephesians 2:11-13, 18-20)

The key to establishing and maintaining **an unshakable faith** is knowing who we are and whose we are in Christ. This is the biblical premise of this book. I have sought to explore some of the vital doctrinal beliefs of the Christian faith in order to push you to your next level in God. It is my prayer that your faith will grow more and more in the knowledge of our God, Jesus Christ, and the Holy Spirit through the transforming power of the Word. There are countless precious promises available to every born-again believer who will study the Word and make it a daily part of their lives. Keep reading— there is abundant life, divine purpose, provision, peace, prosperity, protection, and transforming power in the Word of God. It is a sure foundation for an unshakable faith.

An unknown source said of the Bible, *"The Bible is God's Word to us. It is the traveler's map, the pilgrim's staff, the pilots compass, the soldier's sword and the Christian's charter. It should fill the memory, rule the heart and guide the feet. It should be read slowly, frequently and prayerfully."*

UNSHAKABLE FAITH

CHAPTER 1

UNDERSTANDING OUR CHRISTIAN FAITH
What Is New Testament Theology?

I want to welcome you to a faith journey to refresh your biblical/theological understanding and to rediscover God's Word from a fresh perspective. This can be done through a fresh study of the Bible and what we know as New Testament Theology. There are numerous books, commentaries, periodicals, theological journals, articles and other scholastic materials written on New Testament Theology. Theologians in the church and the seminary have sought ways to understand, teach, preach, and preserve the doctrine of the Christian faith for more than two thousand years.

The vast volumes affirm the reality that no one person or group has a monopoly on the interpretation of either God or His word. The Apostle Peter affirms,

"Knowing this first, that no prophecy of Scripture is of any private interpretation, for prophecy never came by the will of man, but holy men of God spoke as they were moved by the Holy Spirit"
(2 Pet. 1:20-21).

In every age men and women seek to better understand the mysteries of God for every generation. However, God cannot be studied as a science project. All that we know or understand about God is revealed to us by God through the Bible—through anointed persons whom God uses to teach, preach, and prophetically expound on the Word. God also speaks through nature, and other special acts of revelation. God's primary mode of revelation is through the Bible. We understand the word through the inspiration of the Holy Spirit.

In order to grasp the full essence of this study in New Testament Theology, we must first develop a clear understanding of the word theology. The word theology comes from two Greek words—***Theos*** (meaning **God**) and ***logos*** (**meaning study**). Combined the one word means **the study of God.**[1] It is impossible to know or understand God apart from His self-disclosure. Therefore, we rely upon His word as our primary source of understanding. Our theology helps to facilitate our understanding. As a technical discipline, theology is a systematic analysis of God's existence, omnipotence, omnipresence, omniscience, person, attributes, names, works, decrees, and government. In the ancient pagan world, those who knew much about the ancient gods were called **theologians.** This word was simply taken over by the Christian scholars and saints who thought and wrote about God. In that sense, even the authors of the Bible were theologians and what they wrote was theology.[2]

In fact, in some respect, one could say that any Christian is a theologian. What each person thinks about God is his or her theology. The basis of our theology is our understanding of God and His word. The Bible is not just a book of history; it is "His-story" (meaning God's story). It is God's story of His revelation or self-disclosure of Himself in human history. All that we know of God is given by revelation through God's divine resources: the Incarnate Word (Jesus), His inspired word (the Bible), and through general revelation or special revelation. General revelation refers to any disclosure of God that does not rely upon the unrepeatable events of history. This is revelation that God reveals or discloses to all humanity. Special revelation is the divine self-disclosure of God through unique and supernatural events.

Understanding the Theology of the Gospel of Christ

The Christian Gospel is the testimony of God's act of love and redemption in the world as revealed through His Son, Jesus Christ (John 3:16). The word gospel means **good news**. Thus, Christian theology is the attempt to understand and interpret the story of what God has done and is doing in the world. God has confirmed His word and will to us through Jesus Christ as revealed through the Gospels. John H. Sailmaner writes, "Strictly speaking, theology is knowledge of God and divine things." We should add, however, that a theologian not only knows *about* God—a theologian *knows* God. Theology is not a mere set of facts about God; it is knowledge of God that grows out of a relationship with Him. That relationship, for Christian theology, comes through God's word—the written word, the Bible, and the living Word, Jesus Christ.

There is a place for knowing God through His works, such as the created world, but the Bible, the word of God, is the foundation of all Christian theology and the rule of faith. [3]

J. Conyers adds:

> **Theology is the articulation of comprehensive and general truths about God, His creation, and His redemptive actions, based upon (1) the variety in revelation, and (2) the presupposition of the unity of all truth. It is a work that is grounded in the most fundamental of all statements about God, one that was uttered as the fundamental tenet of the Hebrew faith, and without which there would be no Christian faith: "Hear O Israel: The LORD our God is One" (Deut. 6:4). With the oneness of God, thought follows a certain progression: one reality, one world, one humanity, one ethic, and one essential truth. Theology, the idea that one can speak a word (logos) about the one God (theos) and thus come to an understanding of other realities (the world, humanity, sin, redemption, and so on) can only be accomplished on the basis of this fundamental belief in God's oneness.[4]**

One key purpose for writing out our theology or theological understanding about Scripture is as a safeguard against erroneous and defective views. The history of Christian theology is, in fact, a history of fending off erroneous, non-biblical notions about God. Open discussions of theology have thus led to the formation of creeds, that is, succinct statements of theology. The creeds safeguard biblical statements about God from erroneous interpretations. In a sense we could do without theology and creeds if the Bible were never misunderstood.[5]

Our Theological Understanding of God

Throughout human history mankind has sought various ways to interpret and define who God is. The Bible has been divinely inspired (God-breathed) to give us God's Self-revelation through His divine acts in human history. The Holy Bible is the sacred scripture of the Christian Church. This sacred text contains the story of God's intervention in human history through the lives of the Hebrew people. The English word **bible** comes from the Greek and Latin words for **book**. Hence, our Bible contains testimony of both Judaism (the Hebrew Bible) and Christianity (the Old and New Testament) to God's self-revelation to mankind through the Hebrew people and Jesus Christ. The Bible is referred to as the Holy Scripture, not because it contains statements about the nature of God, but because it is the account of the divine-human encounter which took place within human history.[6]

Although the Bible does not argue for the existence of God, His existence is established by God's faithfulness to His promises. The covenant name of God in the Old Testament is Yahweh. The name Yahweh, from the four Hebrew letters **Y-H-W-H**, thus is actually more of a title than a personal name. Since the original Hebrew text did not use vowels, some traditions vocalize the divine name as **J-e-H-o-V-a-H** instead of the more nearly original **Y-a-H-W-e-H**. In English translation, the form usually is rendered The Lord.

In Exodus 3:14, God Affirmed to Moses, *"I AM WHO I AM"* or *"I will be Whom I will be."*

If there were a biblical argument for the existence of God, it might be formulated in this way: God's existence is established by the correspondence of promise and fulfillment.[7] God is faithful to His word. The Bible reminds us that, **"God is not a man that He should lie; neither the son of man that He should repent: hath He spoken, and shall He not make it good?" (Numbers 23:19)** The book of Isaiah gives further confirmation concerning the faithfulness of God's word:

"For My thoughts are not your thoughts, Nor are your ways My ways," says the LORD.

"For as the heavens are higher than the earth, So are My ways higher than your ways, So are My thoughts higher than your thoughts.

For as the rain comes down, and the snow from heaven, and returns not thither, but waters the earth, and makes it bring forth and bud, that it may give seed to the sower and bread to the eater.

So shall my word be that goes out of my mouth: it shall not return unto me void, but it shall accomplish that which I please, and it shall prosper in the thing whereto I sent it." (Isaiah 55:8-11).

The Bible affirms that our God is an awesome God. He is the only true and living God. He commands and demands of us undivided devotion and a whole-hearted faith. Our faith in Him is the key to our strength and success. We must affirm our faith as Paul declared to the philosophers at Athens, ***"for in Him we live and move and have our being"*** (Acts 17:28).

God's Self-Disclosure Through
The Word—The Bible

All knowledge of God comes by way of divine revelation through God's Word, the Bible. The knowledge of God is revealed knowledge since it is God who gives it. The English word Bible comes from the Greek word ***biblio***, meaning "book" or "books." The Bible as we have its complete canonical form is the compilation of at least twelve hundred years—from 1100 BC standing for "before Christ" and AD coming from the Latin *Anno Domini*, meaning "in the year of our Lord." God inspired it to many authors who wrote it in sixty-six books originally on papyrus and parchment and perhaps clay tablets. The Bible is God's inspired Word revealed to us by the Holy Spirit. Paul reminds us that, ***"All Scripture is given by inspiration of God, and is profitable for doctrine, reproof, for correction, for instruction in righteousness*** *(2 Tim.3:16)*. The word *"inspiration"* comes from two Latin words—*in* and **spirare**, *"to breathe."* It means that which is breathed in. The NIV Bible reads, **"All Scripture is God-breathed..."** This breathing of divine revelation and truth is by the Holy Spirit.

Peter further helps us to understand that the Bible and prophetic revelation was not the result of human intuition or human inspiration, but divine revelation. Peter writes, **"For prophecy never had its origin in the will of man, but men spoke from God as they were carried along by the Holy Spirit" (2 Peter 1:2, NIV).** The word "revelation" means "**uncovering, a removal of the veil, a disclosure of what was previously unknown."** More specifically, *revelation is God's manifestation of Himself to humankind in such a way that men and women can know and have fellowship with Him.*

The knowledge of God is revealed knowledge since it is God who gives it. He bridges the gap between Himself and His creatures and discloses Himself and His will to them. God is the source of knowledge about Himself, His ways, and His truth. By God alone can God be known. The knowledge of God is revealed by His self-disclosure.[8] An example of revelation is found in the biblical narrative in which Simon Peter declares that Jesus is the Christ, the Son of the living God (Matt. 16:16). Jesus responded to this declaration by saying to Simon, **"Blessed are you Simon son of Jonah, for this was not revealed to you by man, but my Father in heaven"** (Matt. 16:17).

In this revelatory act, God disclosed Himself—the veil was removed; the gap was bridged. The knowledge of the Son was not attained by human discovery, but by divine revelation. Thus, the foundation of our Christological (Christian) understanding of God is our recognition of God's Self-revelation through the person and work of Jesus Christ. This is the heart of New Testament Theology. This is the essence of our quest to understand God and His revealed Word Jesus Christ, who is "the author and finisher of our faith" (Heb. 12:2). Thus theology is an essential part of our pursuit.

In his book, *Essential Doctrines of the Bible*, David K Bernard writes the following summation concerning God's revelation of Himself through the Bible:

We would expect God to record His message in writing, the historic medium best suited for precision, preservation, and propagation. And the following evidence convincingly demonstrates that the Bible is the unique written Word of God to man: (1) its unique claims, (2) self-vindicating authority, (3) testimony of the apostles and prophets, (4) integrity of Jesus Christ, who endorsed the Old Testament and commissioned the writers of the New, (5) nature and quality of its content, (6) moral superiority, (7) unity, despite more than forty writers over 1,600 years, (8) lack of credible alternative, (9) agreement with history, archeology, and science, (10) indestructibility, (11) universality, (12) influence on society, (13) witness of the Spirit, (14) life-changing power,

(15) fulfilled promises and miracles, (16) fulfilled prophecies, and (17) lack of an alternative explanation for its origin.[9]

In our quest to better understand the Bible in its fuller context, we also use a systematic process known as biblical exegesis. Exegesis is a normal activity in which all of us engage every day of our lives. Whenever we hear an oral statement or read a written one and seek to understand what has been said, we are engaging in exegesis. The term **"exegesis"** comes from the Greek word **exegeomai** which basically meant "to lead out of." When applied to scriptural texts or passages in the Bible, it denotes the "reading out" of the meaning. The noun, therefore, could refer to "interpretation" or "explanation." Thus whenever we read a text or hear a statement which we seek to understand and interpret, we are involved in exegesis.[10]

Exegesis is best thought of as a systematic way of interpreting a text. Biblical exegesis involves the process of critically analyzing a text in its historical, cultural, and literary setting with concern for its grammatical and theological content. In other words, we seek to bridge the historical gap between the original time, setting, and recipients of the message of the text. We then ask critical questions concerning a specific text, such as, what did the text mean to its original recipients and how do we make it relevant to us now? This is the essence of biblical interpretation. We interpret the Bible in order to gain greater insight, spiritual knowledge, and understanding in order that we might live in compliance with God's divine orders. The Bible is our standard rule of faith and practice. We must read it to be wise, and we must practice it to be holy. As regenerated, New Testament believers we concur with the apostle Paul,

"I am crucified with Christ: nevertheless I live; yet not I, but Christ liveth in me: and the life which I now live in the flesh I live by the faith of the Son of God, who loved me, and gave himself for me" (Galatians 2:20).

GOD REVEALED THROUGH HIS
BIBLICAL COVENANT NAMES

In the Old Testament, God not only reveals Himself through His inspired Word, the Bible. He also reveals Himself through His covenant names. Throughout the Old Testament God reveals Himself as *Jehovah, the All-Sufficient Eternal One, the LORD.* When God sent Moses on his liberation mission to Egypt to release the Israelites, Moses said to God:

"Behold, when I come unto the children of Israel, and shall say unto them, The God of your fathers hath sent me unto you; and they shall say to me, What is his name? What shall I say unto them? And God said unto Moses, I AM THAT I AM: and he said, Thus shalt thou say unto the children of Israel, I AM hath sent me unto you." (Ex. 3:13-14)

In many places an explanatory word is added to the name Jehovah to reveal part of His covenant and His character. These names have been fulfilled in the Person of Jesus Christ who claimed the *"I Am"* of the Old Testament in the New Testament. Jesus says, *"before Abraham was born, I am!"* **(John 8:58).** In the Old Testament, God reveals Himself through His covenant names.

The following list conveys God's name and His power through His revealed acts in the lives of His people.

1. *Jehovah-jireh,* the **LORD** *will provide* (Gen. 22:14; Matt. 6:32; Phil. 4:19).

2. *Jehovah-rapha,* the **LORD** *that heals* thee (Ex. 15:26; Matt. 4:23).

3. *Jehovah-nissi,* the **LORD** is *my Banner* (Ex. 17:15; 2 Cor. 12:9-10; Eph. 6:13).

4. *Jehovah-m'kaddesh,* the **LORD** *Who sanctifies* you (Lev.20:8; John 17:19; I Cor. 1:30).

5. *Jehovah-sabbaoth,* the **LORD** *of Host* (Josh. 5:13-15; I Sam. 17:45; Phil. 2:10).

6. *Jehovah-shalom,* the **LORD**, *our Peace* (Judg. 6:22-24; John 14:27).

7. *Jehovah-elyon,* the **LORD** *Most High* **/The Most High GOD** (Ps. 7:17: 83:18; Phil. 2:9: Eph. 1:19-21).

8. *Jehovah-rohi,* the **LORD**, *our Shepherd* (Ps.23:6; John 10:11).

9. ***Jehovah-tsidkenu,*** the **LORD**, *our Righteousness* (Jer. 23:6; Heb. 1:8-9; I Cor. 1:30).

10. ***Jehovah-shammah, the Lord is there*** *(Ezek. 48:35; Matt. 18-20; 2820b).*

~Chapter 1~
Questions for Discussion & Review

1. What is God's primary mode of revelation about himself?

2. What are other ways that God has revealed Himself throughout human history?

3. We understand the Word of God through the inspiration of the
    _____.

4. The word theology comes from two Greek words _____ (meaning God) and _____ (meaning study).

5. Combined, the one word means _____ _____ of _____.

6. The basis of our theology is our understanding of _____ and _____ word.

7. The Bible is God's story of His _____ or _____ of Himself in human history.

8. What is the difference between general revelation and special revelation?

CHAPTER 2

UNDERSTANDING THE PURPOSE AND MESSAGE OF THE NEW TESTAMENT

The New Testament is divided into twenty-seven books. The Bible presents a message about God and His redemptive purposes through grace in human history. God's dealing with people in anticipation of the coming of Christ is the major theme of the thirty-nine Old Testament books. The term "new testament" or "covenant" appears several times in the New Testament. Jesus used it when He instituted the Lord's Supper (see Luke 22:20). With this usage Jesus sought to call attention to the new basis of fellowship with God established by Jesus' sacrificial death and redemptive resurrection. It was God's act of love and redemption that fulfilled His prophetic promise made in the Old Testament. The apostle Paul also spoke of the new covenant (see I Corinthians 11:25; 2 Corinthians 2:14-3:18), as did the author of Hebrews 8:7-13; 9:11-15;10:15-18. The description of God's dealing with people on the basis of the New Covenant is the major theme of the twenty-seven New Testament books.

The Bible tells us, ***"In the past God spoke to our forefathers through the prophets at many times and in various ways, but in these last days he has spoken to us by his***

Son, whom he has appointed heir of all things, through whom he made the universe" (Hebrews 1:1, NIV).

As we read and study the Bible it gives us greater revelation of God's purpose in creation and redemption. It describes the creation of the universe, including the direct creation of man and woman in the paradise of Eden. The Bible describes the fall of man as a direct result of his disobedience to God.

The Bible also tells of the call of Abraham and the patriarchs, the giving of the Law, the establishment of the kingdom, the division of the kingdom, and the captivity and restoration of Israel. The promise of a coming Messiah who will redeem men and women and reign as king appears throughout the Old Testament. The central message of the New Testament is to proclaim God's redemption of sinners through the grace of Jesus Christ. Jesus Christ is the long awaited fulfillment of that prophetic promise. He is the central figure of divine revelation and the focus of the Christian faith.

The New Testament is the authoritative collection of divinely inspired writings of the Christian faith. It is our primary source of doctrine, discipline, and divine directions for Christian living. In the Gospels, we learn that Jesus understood His own life in light of the Scriptures. We also learn that He accepted full authority and divine authorship of the Old Testament. As He taught His disciples in the Sermon on the Mount, the Bible says, ***"the people were astonished at His teachings, for***

He taught as one having authority, and not as the scribes" (Matt. 7:28-29).

The disciples and apostles of Jesus and other apologists of the Christian faith wrote the twenty-seven books that comprise the New Testament. Paul said to Timothy, *"All Scripture is God-breathed and is useful for teaching, rebuking, correcting and training in right-eousness, so that the man of God may be thoroughly equipped for every good work"*(2 Timothy 3:16-17, NIV).

The Fourfold Purpose of the New Testament

1. Its initial purpose is to present, in narrative form, the birth, life, death, and resurrection of Jesus Christ. The Four Gospels each describe events in the life of Jesus. They cite specific Messianic prophecies that show how Jesus' life and death fulfilled Old Testament Promises.

2. The rejection of Jesus by the people of Israel—the Jews of his own day— meant that the kingdom promise in the Old Testament would not be established exactly as foretold. The Book of Acts was written to explain how a fundamentally Jewish remnant of believers in Jerusalem be-

came, in a short time, a primarily Gentile church, spread throughout the ancient world.

3.   The letters of Paul and the other apostles are devoted to the establishment and development of the Gentile churches. These letters were intended to establish guidelines and basic norms for all churches. They became increasingly concerned about doctrine and the problem of false teachers.

4.   The New Testament concludes by focusing on the return of Christ to establish his kingdom on earth.[11]

The work of theology, as Gustaf Aulen stated, is first of all based on a conviction that the Christian faith is by its nature completely theocentric, and thus determined by an act of God in Christ. The presentation of its content must appear as one organic whole.[12]

We must continue to read, study, and seek greater spiritual understanding of the Word of God for our continued spiritual growth and development. The more we know about God, the more we are able to take on His character. His word is transforming when we apply it to our daily lives. We affirm our faith by practicing our faith. We must read the word to be wise, believe it to be safe, and practice it to be holy.

The Focus of Christian Theology

Christian Theology is the attempt to understand and interpret the Christian faith. A systematic or dogmatic theology is the methodical investigation and interpretation of the content of the Christian faith. It is the orderly clarification and explanation of what is affirmed in the Christian message.[13] One then must ask some critical questions:

What role does theology play in the life of the church? Why is it important for the church to study theology or to address the subject of theology? What is the task of the church in each new age?

We must understand that theology is an activity or function of the Christian Church carried out by members of the church. It is the Church reflecting on the basis of its existence and the content of its message. The church has to reflect on its faith and message in every age, so that it can interpret and present them in a way that can be understood in each new period.[14] Therefore, the theological task of the church is to interpret its faith and message so that they can be understood and affirmed in each new age.

As we move swiftly in this new millennium, the Christian Church must seriously reflect on those doctrines that have been held as the foundation of its faith, which is the Bible. We

---

must examine and reflect on these doctrinal beliefs in order to preserve the faith and pass on the Christian testimony to succeeding generations. In the Old Testament, Moses instructed the children of Israel on the divine purpose for reflection and review:

"Now these are the commandments, the statutes, and the judgments, which the LORD thy God commanded to teach you, that you might do them in the land whither you go to possess it. That thou might fear the LORD thy GOD, to keep all His commandments, which I command thee, thou, and thy son, and thy son's son, all the days of thy life that thy days may be prolonged" (Deuteronomy 6:1-2).

The Apostle Paul exhorts Timothy in the New Testament, *"All scripture is given by inspiration of God, and is profitable for doctrine, for reproof, for correction, for instruction (training, discipline) in righteousness, that the man of God may be complete, thoroughly equipped for every good work"* (II Tim.3:16-17). The inspired word is given to equip us with the biblical tools for victorious Kingdom living and service. It is up to us to study and search the Scripture to discover spiritual truth, wisdom, and knowledge that not only sets us free, but also transforms our lives.

In order to be effective we must be people of the Book. We must also be actively engaged in what I call **"Practical Theology."** Practical theology is simply living out our faith daily. We must practice and live by the faith we profess.

We cannot live on faith alone. We must marry our faith with our works. The Bible teaches that faith without works is dead (James 2:17-26). The Bible exhorts us repeatedly to not just be hearers of the word, but also doers of the word. Our purpose, victory, success, power, and prosperity in life are secured through obedience to the Word (Duet. 28; Josh. 1:8). Jesus concluded his "Sermon on the Mount" with a profound illustration through a parable on, the importance of hearing and obeying the word. In the parable he talks about *"the wise"* and *"the foolish" builders.* The man who hears the word and obeys the word is likened to a wise man who built his house on the rocks. The foolish man is one who built his house on the sand. They both experienced storms in their lives, but the man who built his house on the rock was able to withstand the storm. The parable illustrates the importance of building our lives on the Word (See Matt. 7:24-27; James 1:22).

As New Testament believers, we must understand the importance of developing and maintaining practical theology in order to please God. The key to living transformed lives to the glory of God is to continually *"submit our bodies as a living sacrifice, holy, acceptable unto God, which is our reasonable service"* (Romans 12:1-2).

The Theological Mandate of the Christian Church

The Church has a divine mission to speak about God and Jesus Christ to the world. The "Great Commission" is the divine mandate of the Church issued by Christ shortly after His resurrection. The Commission of Christ to His disciples in all ages is this:

"Go therefore, and teach all nations, baptizing them in the name of the Father, and the name of the Son, and in the name of the Holy Ghost; Teaching them to observe all things whatsoever I have commanded you: and lo, I am with you always even to the end of the world. Amen."(Matthew 28:19-20)

This Commission serves as the theological mandate of the Church to share its faith and theology with the world through worship, preaching, teaching, fellowship, Christian Education, local and foreign missions, evangelistic outreach ministries, and living out our faith daily. I call this "life style evangelism."

The Christian Church has an urgent mission to proclaim Christ to the end of the ages. Our Christian theology helps us to clarify our Gospel message to make it clear and accessible to people of all colors, cultures and all continents. Shortly before His ascension, Jesus instructed His disciples, *"But you shall receive power after that the Holy Spirit has come upon you; and you shall be my witnesses in Jerusalem, in all Judaea and Samaria, and the uttermost parts of the earth" (Acts 1:8).*

This is not the task of a few faithful saints in the church, but it is the total responsibility of every born-again believer in Christ. We must proclaim the gospel of a cosmic Christ and His saving grace to all humanity. ***Too many Christian are satisfied being sanctified sitting in the sanctuary.*** They have no burden for reaching the lost, lonely, and left out. Many Christians in our churches are more concerned about their sacred cows, traditions, special days, and their personal prosperity. They have forgotten that we also have a mandate to help reach others for Christ. God has no problem with us being blessed and prosperous. We have to understand that in the economy of God, we are blessed to be a blessing to others. We are not blessed to hoard our wealth. We are blessed to share our financial resources, witness, and sow into the ministry for the expansion of God's Kingdom Agenda. We have a divine mandate for both local and global ministry and missions. Failure to do so is a poor testament to our Christian faith.

Owen C. Thomas makes reference regarding the mission of the Church. It uses its language about God in all of its activities, in worship, preaching, instruction, social action, and pastoral care. The function and task of theology is to test, criticize, and revise the language which the Church uses about God—to test it by norm, namely, God's self-disclosure to which testimony is given in the Bible. This testing is necessary because the church's language about God is fallible and can fall into error and confusion.[15]

Why Is Theology Necessary In The Life Of The Church?

The Church's understanding of God and the gospel is always being expanded and deepened. Therefore, we must ask the question, why is theology necessary in the life of the church? O.C. Owens offers four reasons for this necessity.

1.   Theology is necessary in the life of the church in order to determine what is essential to the Christian faith and message and what is peripheral. In a word, theology is necessary in order to determine what is and what is not part of the Christian faith.

2.   Secondly, after preaching there must be teaching in the church—catechetical instruction—explaining what the Christian faith means and requires. The simplest kind of teaching, even to the youngest children, is full of theological content. There are several references in the New Testament to the necessity of teaching and teachers.

3.   The Bible as the main source and standard of Christian teaching is not uniform. It does not present a simple unity of teaching but rather a multiplicity of different approaches which must be resolved by critical reflection and by theological work. We cannot require modern people to return to the thought world of the first century nor can we present the thought world of the Bible untranslated. Thus, the work of theology is essential.

4.   The Christian message, which is based on the Bible, must be distinguished from the scientific picture of the world of the first century.[16]

~*Chapter 2*~
Questions for Discussion & Review

1. What is the primary message of the New Testament?

2. Describe the central theological basis for communicating the Gospel?

3. What is the fourfold purpose of the New Testament?

4. How do we affirm our faith as Christian believers?

5. What is the primary focus of Christian Theology?

6. What is "Practical Theology" as defined in this chapter?

7. Why is theology necessary in the life of the Church?

CHAPTER 3

DEVELOPING A GREATER UNDERSTANDING ABOUT THE THEOLOGY OF CHRIST— *CHRISTOLOGY*

In order to develop a clear understanding of New Testament Theology, we must begin our quest with the doctrine of Christ. This section concerns the Lord Jesus Christ—the central theme of NT Scripture. We shall consider His deity, His work, and His offices. One of the foundational truths of the Christian faith is that Jesus Christ is truly God and that He came into the world as a man by the miracle of virgin birth. The Good News of the Gospel of Christ involves the whole story of Christ, including his supernatural conception and birth through the Virgin Mary. We also believe that Christ is the Son of God according to the Scripture. The Bible teaches, ***"In the beginning was the Word, and the Word was with God, and the Word was God. The same was in the beginning with God" (John 1:1-2).***

The central message proclaimed in the Bible and understood theologically in the New Testament is that believers are restored to favor with God through the sacrifice of Jesus Christ. His sacrifice puts an end to the Old Testament sacrificial system in which the blood of animals served as a method of atonement for sins. The New Testament reveals how Christ has come into the world to be the Living Lamb. John the Baptist declared of Jesus, ***"Behold the Lamb of***

***God who takes away the sins of the world"
(John 1:29).***

Throughout the New Testament, the Bible bears witness of Christ's redemptive work for the sins of the world. The New Testament also reveals the Christ who brought salvation and describes how these prophecies about Him were minutely fulfilled. This unifying message ties the biblical library together. A.J. Conyers writes, "The Old Testament promises were fulfilled in the New Testament message of the gospel and affirms that Jesus is the central figure of divine revelation and the focus of the Christian faith."[17]

When we study the four Gospels, particularly the Sermon on the Mount in Matthew 5-7, we discover that Jesus made several references to Himself as the fulfillment of the Old Testament. He said affirmatively and authoritatively, ***"Think not that I am come to destroy the law, or the prophets: I am not come to destroy, but to fulfill" (Matthew 5:17).*** Jesus spoke with such authority that it baffled the minds of His hearers. The Bible says, ***"And it came to pass, when Jesus had ended these sayings, the people were astonished at His doctrine: For he taught them as one having authority, and not as the scribes" (Matthew 7:29).*** Christ's authority validates his divinity as God and Man. He is God incarnate. He is both "the Son of God" and "the Son of man" manifested among us.

I. HIS DEITY

The deity of Christ means that Christ is God. This is one of the unique distinctions of our Christian faith. It is also one of the key points of disagreement which many other world religions refuse to accept. We believe that Jesus is in fact the Son of God and that He is one with God. In the Gospel According to John, the Bible teaches us a valuable lesson about the deity of Christ with God:

"In the beginning was the Word, and the Word was with God, and the Word was God. The same was in the beginning with God. All things were made by him; and without him was not any thing made that was made."
(John 1:1-4)

These verses help us to understand Christ's deity as creator of the world. Scripture clearly teaches this important fact in the following ways.

A. The Attributes of God Used in Speaking of Christ.

1. **Pre-existence:** Christ has no beginning (John 17:5; 9:1-7)

2. **Omnipresence:** He is with His servants everywhere (Matthew 28:20)

3. **Omnipotence**: He has unlimited power (Revelation 1:18; Matthew 28:19)

4. **Omniscience**: He has unlimited knowledge (John 21:17)

5. **Unchangeableness**: He is the same, yesterday, today and forever (Hebrews 13:8)

B. The Works of God Were Performed By Christ.

1. He created all things (John 1:3).

2. He upholds the universe (Colossians 1:16).

3. He raised Himself from the dead (John 20:1-31; Matthew 28:1-10; Luke 24; Mark 16).

C. Titles of God Are Given To Christ.

1. God the Father addresses the Son as God (Hebrews 1:8).
2. Men called Him God, and He did not refuse their worship (John 20:28).
3. Demons recognized Him as God (Mark 1:24).

4. He declared Himself to be God
(John 10:30).

II. HIS INCARNATION (*Incarnation means God in human flesh.*)

A. The coming of Christ was predicted in the Old Testament. (Isaiah 7:14)

B. History records the birth of our Lord. His birth was different from all other births:

1. The Holy Ghost supernaturally conceived Jesus (Luke 1:35).

2. He was born of a virgin named Mary (Matthew 1:23).

3. Yet He was truly man, possessing a body, soul, and spirit (Hebrews 10: 5; Matthew 26:38; Luke 23:46).

C. Christ came in human form in order to:

1. Reveal God the Father (John 14:9).

2. Put away sin by His sacrificial death (Hebrews 9:26).

3. Destroy the works of the devil (I John 3:8).

III. HIS   WORK

A. **His Death**. The Scriptures affirm the necessity of Christ's death in several significant ways:

1. **The Death of Christ Was Necessary As A Ransom for Our Sins** (Matt. 20:28; I Pet. 1:18; I Tim. 2:6: Gal. 3:13; John 3:14).
    It was part of God's eternal purpose (Hebrews 10:7).
    It was necessary to fulfill Old Testament prophecies (Isaiah 53:5; Luke 24:27, 44; I Pet. 1:11, 12).
    It was necessary to provide salvation for man.

2. **As A Propitiation (Mercy Seat or Covering) for Our Sins**. He died as a substitute. The mercy-seat covering the Ark of the Covenant was called propitiation (Exod. 25:22; Heb. 9:5; I Cor.15:3).

3. **The Death of Christ Was Sufficient For Our Reconciliation.**
    It completely meets God's claim because Christ endured and exhausted the judgment of God against sin and restored us to right fellowship with God (Rom. 5:1-10; 2 Cor. 5: 17-18; Eph. 2:16; Col. 1:20).
    It completely meets man's need because it

was the death of an infinite Person and therefore its value is infinite.

4. **The Death of Christ Was Necessary As A Substitution for Us**
(Isa. 53:1-12; 2 Cor. 5:21; I Pet. 2:24; 3:18)
Christ's death on the cross is the New Testament embodiment of the Old Testament story of the Passover lamb (Exod. 12).

B. The Power of Christ's Resurrection

1. The resurrection of Christ was necessary to fulfill prophecy, to complete the work of the cross, and to enable Christ to undertake His present work in heaven. (Romans 4:25)

2. Christ's resurrected body was real. It was not a spirit (Luke 24:39). It was the same body that was crucified, because as He revealed himself to his disciples, he showed them the print of the nails in his hands and the spear wound in his side (John 20:27). Yet, it was a changed body, with power to over-come physical limitations. This means it was a glorified body.

3. After His resurrection, Christ appeared to some of His followers at least ten times. More than five hundred reliable witnesses saw Him after He arose. (I Corinthians 15:6)

4. The resurrection of Christ is one of the central pillars of the Christian faith. We believe that God raised Jesus from the dead according to Scripture. This is the key to saving faith according to Roman 10:1-17. If there had been no resurrection, there would be no Christian faith.

C. His Ascension.

1. At the end of His ministry on earth, Christ was carried up into heaven (Mark 16:19; Acts 1:9).

2. He ascended so that He might enter in His reward and continue His ministry for His people (John 17:5; Heb. 12:1-2).

3. Continues His ministry of intercession (John 17:5; Heb.12:1-2).

D. His Second Advent/ Return
Matthew 24:27-51
Acts 1:10-11
I Thessalonians 4:13-17

IV. HIS OFFICES

Christ is presented in Scripture as a Prophet, Priest, King, and Apostle.

A. As **Prophet**, He tells men what God has to say to them, and He thus reveals God to men (John 1:18; Matt. 13:57; 7:11- 28; 8:9).

B. As **Priest**, He represents believers before God Hebrews 3:1-11; 4:14-16; 7; 8; 9).

C. As **King**, He reigns today in the hearts of those who are loyal to Him. In a coming day, He will reign upon the earth for one thousand years (Matt.2:2; 27:37; John19:14; I Tim. 1:17; 6:15; Rev.19:16).

D. As **Apostle**, He was sent on assignment from the Father to establish a New Testament paradigm or model for spiritual leadership and ministry (Heb. 3:1; Eph. 4:11-14; Rom 1:1-6).

~*Chapter 3*~
Questions for Discussion & Review

1. What is another word for the theology of Christ?

2. What do we mean theologically by the Deity of Christ?

3. What are at least three major attributes of God used in speaking about the character of Christ?

4. What is meant by the Incarnate of Christ?

5. What are four primary offices of Christ according to Scripture?

6. Briefly describe each of these offices.

CHAPTER 4

UNDERSTANDING THE DOCTRINE OF THE HOLY SPIRIT-PNEUMATOLOGY

One of the great mysteries of New Testament Theology is the understanding of the Person and work of the Holy Spirit. Often people have referred to the Holy Ghost or Holy Spirit as an abstract object or thing. Referring to Him as "it". Even in many of our Christian songs, our theology about the Holy Spirit is incorrect. However, we must understand and affirm that the Holy Spirit is the third Person of the Godhead known as the Trinity (Father, Son and Holy Spirit). The term Trinity is not found in the Bible. It gives reference to the unique relationship between the tri-unity, or three-ness, of God. Early reference to the Spirit of God in the Old Testament helps us to understand the New Testament background.

In the Old Testament, the Holy Spirit wrought upon the hearts of men in many ways. The Holy Spirit was present in creation, bringing the present cosmos out of chaos. His presence was manifested throughout the Bible in the lives of certain individuals, such as priests, prophets, and kings in Israel. We find the term Holy Spirit in Psalm 51:11 and Isaiah 63:10-11. In Psalms 51, David prays, ***"Create within me a clean heart, O God. And renew a right spirit within me. Do not cast me away from Your presence, And do not take Your Holy Sprit from*** *me" (Psalms 51:11-12).* Isaiah 63 says, *"But they rebelled and grieved his Holy Spirit."*

Two particular metaphors are used in the Old Testament to describe the presence of God or the Spirit. One is **"neshemah"**, meaning **"breath"**. The other is **"ruach"**, meaning **"wind"**. These terms are translated in the New Testament with the Greek term **pneuma, "air".** Thus the doctrine of the Holy Spirit is called **Pneumatology.** Whether *"breath,"* *"wind"* or *"air,"* we know that the words we use for spirit imply a certain connection of intimacy and mystery.[18]

The Person, Power, and Purpose of the Holy Spirit

The Holy Spirit is the eternal Spirit of God Himself. The Spirit is the same in the Old Testament as He is in the New Testament. Jesus clarifies our understanding by teaching that, *"God (in His essential being) is a Spirit and they that worship him must worship Him in spirit and in truth" (John 4:24).* God's Spirit, the Holy Spirit, is His very self, not merely an attribute or function of God. To know God is to know His Spirit. To worship God means that we worship Him as the Word teaches **"in Spirit and in truth."**

The Holy Spirit is a Person, not an abstract as we previously mentioned. He is referred to by the pronoun *He* and is spoken of in terms of His personality characteristics on numerous occasions in the New Testament. The Holy Spirit is often identified in the New Testament as the Spirit of Christ. On several occasions in the Gospel of John, Jesus made reference that the role of the Holy Spirit is to bear witness of Christ. The Holy Spirit glorifies Christ and points us to Christ:

"And I will pray the Father, and He shall give you another Comforter (Helper, Greek 'paraclete'), that he may abide with you forever; Even the Spirit of truth..." *(John 14:16);* *"When the Comforter comes... he will testify about me"* *(John 15:26);* *"He will not speak on his own; he will speak only what he hears...He will bring glory to me"* *(John 16:13-14).*

One of the primary responsibilities of the Holy Spirit in the world is to bring glory to Christ. He continues to focus our attention on Christ and His redemptive work in the world. This does not devalue the person of the Holy Spirit; rather it shows His apostolic role in the Kingdom of God in teaching us and leading us into all truth.

Holy Spirit's Unity with God the Father

Trinity   Matt. 28:19
Omnipresent   Psalm 139:7
Omniscient   I Cor. 2:10
Omnipotent   Matt. 12:18
Benediction Formula 2 Cor. 13:14

The Work of the Holy Spirit

The work of the Holy Spirit is multifaceted. In our quest for greater theological understanding, it is imperative that we understand the Person and work of the Holy Spirit in the life of every born-again believer.

He Leads to Salvation. The Holy Spirit convicts of sin, righteousness, and judgment (John 16:11). His work is to lead persons to conviction of their sins, to their need for Christ's righteousness as their only hope, and to the fact of impending judgment if they do not repent by turning to the Savior.

He Indwells the Believer. The indwelling of the Holy Spirit is not an experience apart from salvation; every born-again believer is indwelt by the Spirit at the moment of conversion (John 7:37-38). The whole new birth or regeneration process of salvation is the Holy Spirit transforming the believer as a child of God (John 3:1-6; Romans 8:9; I Cor. 12: 3). The Holy Spirit indwells every born-again believer as Christ's presence in us and with us. This indwelling provides power, discipline, and direction for Christ-centered living. He enables the believer to develop the Character of Christ.

He Baptizes With Power and Authority. One of the enabling works of the Spirit is to baptize the believer to walk in the same power that Christ operated in (Matt.3:11; John 1:33). The Spirit also gives delegated authority to operate as Christ representatives in the world (Luke 9:1-2; 10:1-20). Prior to His ascension, Jesus confirmed the promise of the baptism of the Holy Spirit (Acts 1:4-5).

He Sanctifies the Believer. The act of salvation is instantaneous, but sanctification is a continuous process. The Holy

Spirit may sanctify an individual at the moment of Salvation, but His abiding work in that person's life is a daily process (I Cor. 6:9).

He Leads the Church. The Book of Acts of the Apostles tells of the powerful presence and work of the Holy Spirit in the life of the New Testament Church in the first century. In Acts 1:8, Jesus informs the disciples about the baptism of the Holy Spirit. In Acts 2, tells of the powerful filling that occurred in the upper room on the Day of Pentecost.

He is our Comforter/Counselor (Gr. **Paraclete**, *parakletos*-John 14:16, 26). The Bible speaks of the Holy Spirit as Comforter or Counselor. The Greek word for counselor is Paraclete. This word is sometimes used for lawyer. It means one who is called along side of or who walks along side of. Jesus said the Holy Spirit will "abide with us forever" (John 14:16).

He is our Teacher (John 14:26). As we pointed out earlier, one of the primary roles of the Holy Spirit is to teach us about Christ. The Spirit is our teacher as we seek to know Christ. He does not place emphasis on Himself but on Christ. He teaches us also how to recognize the things of God as He speaks to us in various ways. He gives spiritual discernment in order that we might know the deep mysteries of God (I Cor. 2:4-16).

The Spirit not only teaches us to recognize truth, He also "guides us into all truth" (John 16:12-16).

Other Works of the Holy Spirit Include:

Witness
John 15:26

Personality
John 16:13

Procession
John 15:26

Conviction
John 16:8

Intercessor
Romans 8:26-27

Baptism of the Holy Spirit
I Cor. 12:13

Sealing
Eph. 1:13, 14

Sign Gifts
Heb. 2:4

Spiritual Gifts (Serving gifts)
I Cor. 7:7; 12; Ro. 12

Fullness of the Holy Spirit
Eph. 5:18

Anointing
I John 2:27

Outpouring
Acts 2:1-18

Fruits
Gal. 5:22,23

Empowering for Effective Witness
Acts1:8

Sins Against the Holy Spirit

Lying to the Holy Spirit
Acts 5:1-3

Resisting the Holy Spirit
Acts 7:51

Quenching the Holy Spirit
I Thess. 5:19

Grieving the Holy Spirit
Eph. 4: 30

Biblical References
on Being Filled with the Holy Spirit

A realization of a personal need
John 7:37-39

A Holy Desire
John 7:37-39

Repentance
Acts 2:38

A holy conviction wrought in the soul
through the Word
John 7:38; Romans 10:17

Faith in the Word
Romans 10:17; John 7:38

A sincere willingness to renounce and
abandon all known sin
Luke 9:23; Galatians 2:20

A whole-hearted surrender of self to the
flow of the Spirit
John 7:37-39

UNSHAKABLE FAITH

~Chapter 4~
Questions for Discussion & Review

1. What is the Greek word for the study of the Holy Spirit?

2. Briefly describe the connection of the Holy Spirit to God the Father and God the Son.

3. Briefly describe some of the works the Holy Spirit does in the life of born-again believers.

4. Why is it vitally important that we need to know the Person, Power, and Purpose of the Holy Spirit?

5. What are some biblical sins against the Holy Spirit?

6. Highlight some of the biblical references for being filled with the Holy Spirit.

7. How does the Holy Spirit help or assist us in understanding the Bible?

8. How does the Holy Spirit help us in prayer warfare according to the Word? (Romans 8:26; Jude 20).

9. Think of some ways the Holy Spirit has helped you in your personal faith walk with Christ and list them.

CHAPTER 5

UNDERSTANDING OTHER FUNDAMENTAL DOCTRINES OF THE CHRISTIAN FAITH

The Doctrine of Man

The Doctrine of Man tells us about man's creation, nature, and original relationship with God, relation to other beings, his fall, and God's sovereign act of redemption and ultimate destiny. Martin Luther said, "The doctrine of creation is the foundation of the whole of Scripture." It is essential to our Christian faith that we understand what we believe. The evolutionists teach Charles Darwin's Theory that man evolved. But we affirm the biblical report: ***"In the beginning God created the heavens and the earth" (Genesis 1:1).*** We believe according to the Scripture:

God said, Let us make (create) man in our image, after our likeness: and let them have dominion over the fish of the sea and over the fowl of the air, and over every creeping thing. So God created man in His own image, in the image of God created him; male and female created them." (Gen. 1:26 -27)

Let me put a footnote here on the fact that the Bible says, ***"male and female created them."*** There is a great deal of satanically induced doctrine from the homosexual community/ pro-gay community who argues that same-sex marriage is permissible by God. This doctrine is even promoted by some in the religious community that same-sex marriage, alternative lifestyles, and sexual preference is biblically acceptable behavior. But that is as far from the truth as Heaven is from hell.

As God-fearing, Christ-centered, Bible-Based Believers, we must take a bold definitive stand on our faith conviction that we affirm God's order for man and woman. We cannot waiver in neutrality nor can we be silent in this matter. We must be definitive on what the Bible teaches without compromising our faith conviction or values with the twisted doctrine of the world.

Creation **Gen. 1:27**
Soul **Gen. 2:7**
Image and Likeness of God **Gen. 1:26**
The Fall of Man **Gen. 3**
Immaterial Part of Man **Heb. 4: 12**
Heart **Proverbs 4:23**
Conscience **Ro. 2:15**
Temptation **I John 2:16**
Headship of Adam **Ro. 5:12**
Marriage **Gen. 2:24**
Divorce **Matt. 19:3**

The Doctrine of Sin

Sin is a theological concept. A theological understanding of sin is a falling away from or missing the mark. It is disobeying the divine order, law, or will of God. The Bible affirms **"all unrighteousness is sin"** (I John 5: 17). Paul declares, **"all have sinned and come short of the glory of God"** (Ro. 3:23). The Bible also teaches, **"The wages of sin is death; but the gift of God is eternal life through Jesus Christ our Lord"** *(Rom. 6:23).*

The NT also describes sin as actions contrary to God's expressed will (James 4:12, 17). The Greek NT has a dozen or more terms for sin. The word used most often is **hamartia,** meaning "to transgress, to do wrong, to sin against God, or to miss the mark" The concept of sin presupposes an absolute law, given by an absolute lawgiver, God. Therefore, many who do not believe God exists do not believe such a thing as sin exists. (See Heb. 11:1, 6).

The Christian doctrine of sin has two aspects. First, we are born sinful and our sinfulness gives rise to sinful acts. We are not sinful because we sin; rather we sin because we are sinful. Secondly, we believe that Christ died that we may not perish in our sins, which distinguishes Christianity from all other world religions that do not believe that humankind is innately sinful. Sin separated us from God; it was Christ who came to reconcile us back to God:

"Therefore if any man be in Christ, he is a new creature: old things are passed away; behold, all things are become new. And all things are of God who has reconciled us to Himself by Jesus Christ, and has given us the ministry of reconciliation" (2 Cor. 5:17-18).

Because we are now in Christ, it is our Christian duty to reach the world for Christ with our personal and corporate witness. In other words, we confess our theological faith, we preach, teach, and live it daily.

The Fall of Man as a Result of sin
Gen. 3:14-19

Personal Sin
Ro. 3:23; I Cor. 6:9; Gal. 6:1; I Tim. 4:2

Sin Nature
Ps. 51:5; Eph. 2:3

Imputed
Ro. 5: 12

Apostasy
2 Thess. 2:3

Pollution of Sin
I Cor. 5:6

Penalty of Sin
Ro. 6:23

Struggle of Sin
Ro. 7

Flesh
Ro. 8:13

Doctrine of Salvation Soteriology

The theological term Soteriology comes from two Greek words: ***soteria,*** "safety," and logos, "the study of." Soteriology is the branch of theology that studies salvation. It examines the provisions of salvation through Jesus Christ and its practical application through the Holy Spirit, including such topics as the fall and sin, God's revelation, and God's redemption of people by means of Christ's crucifixion, the atonement, and grace.[19]

The main work of Christ as presented in the Gospels is salvation and the redemption of humanity: ***"For the Son of man is come to seek and to save that which was lost"*** *(Luke 19:10).* Salvation is wholly the result of God's grace to us. This fact is proclaimed throughout the NT: ***"For God so love the world, that He gave His only begotten Son, that whosoever*** *believes in him should not perish, but have everlasting life. For God sent not His Son into the world to condemn the world; but that the world through him might be saved. He that believes in him is not condemned: but he that believes not is condemned already, because he has not believed in the name of the only begotten Son of God"* (John 3:16).

Paul makes it theologically clear that we are **saved by the grace** of God:

"For by grace you are saved, through faith; and that not of yourselves: it is the gift of God" (Eph. 2:8). The Greek word for grace is **charis**, which speaks of God's redemptive love. Grace also means favor, thanks, goodwill, and gratitude. Salvation is an all-encompassing experience which includes three dimensions: becoming a believer in Jesus Christ at the point of decision, the continuing life of discipleship, and final redemption.[20]

Regeneration (New Birth)- John 3:1-15

Conversion- Ro. 6:17

Repentance- Luke 13:3

Justification by faith- Ro. 5

Confession of salvation- Ro.10:1-21

Saved by Grace- Eph. 2:8

Reconciliation- 2 Cor. 5:17-20

Propitiation- Ro. 3:25

Redemption- I Pet. 1:18,19

Substitutionary Death- Ro.5:8

Forgiveness of Sins- Eph.1:7

Adoption- Eph.1:5

Security of Believers- John 10:28

Priesthood of Believers- I Pet. 2:9

Union with Christ- John 15

New Creation- 2 Cor. 5:17; I Cor. 6:9-11

Crucified with Christ- Gal. 2:20

The Theology of the Church-Ecclesiology

A clear theological understanding of the Church is also vital to our faith journey and Christian living. As regenerate baptized believers in Christ, we are a part of the greatest institution in the world. But the Church is more than an institution, "it is a spiritual organism, birthed, founded, and ordained by Christ Himself. The Bible teaches us, **"For the husband is the head of the wife, even as Christ is the head of the Church"** *(Ephesians 5:23).* The word *church* is a transliteration of the compound Greek word *ekklesia,* also rendered *ecclesia.* The word *Ekklesia* is made up of the preposition *ek* (out of) and the verb *kaleo* (to be called). The word which appears more than one hundred time in the New Testament refers to an assembly that has been gathered for a specific purpose. The Greeks used the word to refer to a body of citizens who were *called out* and gathered to discuss the affairs of the town or state (see Acts 19:39). It was often used to refer to the political assembly in a Roman city-state.

In the Septuagint, it is used to designate the gathering of Israel, summoned for any definite purpose, or a gathering as representatives of the whole nation. When used in the New Testament, it refers to the called-out ones, called out from sin to salvation, from death to life, from hell to heaven, from slavery to Satan to serve the

Savior, and from the bondage of spiritual darkness to the liberty of the Holy Spirit. The Church is comprised of those who have been summoned by God to worship and serve Him.

The concept of the church runs throughout Paul's theological and doctrinal writings. This is attributable to at least two reasons: his relation to the revelation of the mystery of the Body accounts for his concept of the church universal and his desire to organize his converts into self-governing and self-propagating groups accounts for the emphasis on the local church.[21]

The word church is used in two primary perspectives in the New Testament. First, it refers to the local assembly. Secondly, it refers to the universal church (Body of Christ). The Church is also composed of what has been called the **Visible** and the **Invisible** Church. The Church Visible is composed of all those who are members of the local church regardless of denominational preference. The Invisible Church is composed of those who are members of the universal body of regenerate believers born into the Kingdom of God by faith in Christ.

Jesus told Nicodemus in order to see or enter the Kingdom, one must be born again of the water and the Spirit. These are those who have confessed and believed on the name of the Lord Jesus as their personal Savior. They have united with the citizens of Heaven. Peter describes the believers as more than just members of a religious organization called a Church. Peter helps us to understand that we are a chosen generation, a royal priesthood, a holy nation, peculiar people, that should show forth the praises of Him who called us out of darkness and into the marvelous light—which in time past were not a people, but are now the people of God, which had not obtained mercy, but have now obtained mercy (I Peter 2:9-10).

> ## The Foundation of the Church is Christ-Matt. 16:18; Eph. 2:17-22

The Bible helps us to better understand the foundation of the Church in Jesus' discourse in Matthew 16:18. In this familiar passage, Jesus asked his disciples a question regarding His identity. He asked, Who do men say that I am, to which He received several responses: *"Some say that you are John. Others say that you are Elijah, or one of the other prophets."* Jesus then asked a more personal question: *"Who do you say that I am?"* Peter responded, *"thou are the Christ the son of the living God."* To this response Jesus declared,

"And I say unto you..... Upon this rock, I will build my Church; and the gates of hell shall not prevail against it" (Matthew 16:18).

In Ephesians, Paul reminds us that as believers we *"are built upon the foundation of the apostles and prophets, Jesus Christ being the chief cornerstone or foundation stone"* (Ephesians 2:17-22). Because our faith is built upon the eternal truth of Christ, our foundation is sure and steadfast. We have an eternal heritage with the Father through Jesus the Son. All who are a part of this eternal family are sealed until the day of redemption through the Holy Spirit of promise (Ephesians 1:13).

Other Theological References Regarding the Church

Spiritual Discipline for Growth
Acts 2

Five-Fold Equipping Gifts
Eph. 4:11-14

Purpose and Missionary Mandate
Matt. 28:19-20

Fellowship
Acts 2:42; Philippians 1:27; Heb. 10:25

Baptism in Christ
Romans 6:4

Lord's Supper
I Corinthians 11:20

Foot Washing
John 13:10

Qualifications of a Bishop/Pastoral Office
I Tim. 3:1

Qualifications of Deacons
I Tim. 3:8

Ordination
Acts 13:3

Church and State
Matt. 22: 21

Bride of Christ
Eph. 5:32

Body of Christ
I Cor. 12:27

The Doctrine of Last Things— *Eschatology*

The theological doctrine that refers to biblical end time prophetic events is referred to as Eschatology. Eschatology comes from the Greek *eschatos,* "the last, last things," and **logos**, "the study of."[22] Roy T. Edgemon makes reference: "The Bible presents human history as moving toward a divinely directed goal. History is not cyclical, with events recurring in an eternal cycle, nor is it evolutionary, progressing under its own power. Rather, it is moving in a direction determined by God. It will reach the goal that He has ordained."[23]

All Christians do not believe the same things in this vital doctrinal area. But even though various viewpoints about the future are held, all Christians believe that God is at work in history, that Jesus Christ will return, and that those who know Him will share in His glory. The goal toward which history is moving is expressed in Revelation 11:15: ***"The kingdom of the world has become the kingdom of our Lord and of his Christ, and he will reign for ever and ever."***

Significant Scripture References

Signs of Christ's Return
Matt. 24; 33

Dispensation and Covenants
Eph. 3:2

Fullness of Time
Eph. 1:10

Kingdom Parables
Matt. 13:1-52

Rapture
I Thess. 4:17

Character of the Great Tribulation
Matt. 24:21

Seventy Weeks
Daniel 9:24

Times of the Gentiles
Luke 21:24

Anti-Christ
I John 2:22

False Prophet
Rev. 13:11

Second Coming of Christ
Rev.19:11

Judgments
Rev. 2:1-16

Death
Rev. 20:15

Torments
Luke 16:23

Wrath of God
Rom.1:18

Heaven
John 14:2

The Theology of Angels—*Angelology*

The doctrine of angels is one that is not discussed directly as some of the other specific theological doctrines. The Bible does not present a specific doctrine of angels as it does about God, Christ, the Holy Spirit, and the doctrine of Humanity. However, it is very much a part of New Testament theological beliefs. In both the Old and New Testaments, the root word for angel means **"messenger."** The Hebrew word **mal'akh** in the Old Testament and the Greek word *angelos* in the New Testament mean simply "messenger." The word can refer to a human or to a created spiritual or supernatural being whose purpose is to serve God as His messenger or ambassador. Angels are the elect ambassadors or emissaries of God (I Timothy 5:21).[24]

The importance of both the Hebrew *mal'akh* and Greek *angelos* for the study of angels is that both terms describe the function or duty of angels rather than their nature. That is, the nomenclature describes an office rather a nature; they tell us what angels do rather than what they are. The Bible assumes throughout that God is attended by a company or host of heavenly beings who are subordinate to Himself and who share His company and reflect His glory and majesty as in Isaiah 6. The supernatural beings we call "angels" were present at creation (Job 38:7). They seem to be ranked in a hierarchy, for some are called "archangels" (I Thess. 4:16; Jude 9). Some scholars feel Jude 6 suggests that there has been a fall of angels.

Angels in the New Testament

The Angel Gabriel Announces the Birth of John the Baptist **Luke 1:8-9, 11-13**

The Angel Gabriel Announces the Birth of Christ **Luke 1:27-28, 30-31**

Angels Announce to the Shepherds the Birth of Christ **Luke 2:8-15**

Angels Minister to Christ After His Temptation **Matthew 4:1-11; Mark 1:13**

An Angel Strengthened Christ in His Agony at Gethsemane **Luke 22:43-44**

Angels Were Witnesses and Heralds of Christ's Resurrection **Matthew 28:2-7; Luke 24:23; John 20:11-14**

Angels Attended Christ at His Ascension **Acts 1:3**

Angels Are to Accompany Christ at His Second Advent
I Thessalonians 4:16; 2 Thessalonians 1:7-9

Angels Minister to Believers **Heb. 1:14; Acts 12:7; Acts 27:23-24**

Angels Minister to Unbelievers **Acts 12:23; Matt. 13:39**

Ranking of Angels **Heb. 12: 22**

An Angel Delivers the Apostles from Prison **Acts 5:19**

An Angel Instructs Cornelius **Acts 10:1-3**

An Angel Releases Peter from Prison **Acts 12:6-7**

Satan—A Fallen Angel **Is. 14:12**

Angels Executing Judgment **Rev. 8; 9; 16**

~Chapter 5~
Questions for Discussion & Review

1. What is the theological understanding of the Doctrine of Man?

2. What is the theological understanding for the Doctrine of Sin?

3. What is the Theology of Salvation?

4. What is the Greek term used for the Theology of the Church?

5. What is Eschatology?

6. What is another name for Angel?

Glossary of Key Theological Terms

Agape- The word that describes the love of God. It denotes God's relationship to both individuals and groups.

Angel- From the Greek *angelos,* literally "a messenger." The term can refer to a human or a created spiritual or supernatural being whose purpose is to serve God as His messenger or ambassador.

Angelology- The study or doctrine of angels. Angelogy is the area of Christian theology that deals with clarifying and systematizing beliefs about the existence, nature, and function of angels.

Biblical Theology - The attempt to understand and interpret the teachings of the Bible as a whole.

Charisma, charismata- Grace gift, gifts of the Spirit, provided to the church for the sake of fulfilling its calling and ministering to one another.

Christ- From the Greek word ***Christos***, "the Anointed One." The title designates Jesus as the Messiah.

Christocentric- A system of thought or practices in which Christ has the central or dominant place.

Christology- From the Greek words ***Christos,*** Christ and ***logos***, the rational study of. In theology, it refers to the study of the doctrine of Christ centering on His life, person, works, faith, significance, and divinity. The doctrine of Christ.

Church-In the NT, the Greek word ***ekklesia*** is translated "church." The church is "the called out."

Cosmology- From the Greek word ***cosmos*** (world) and ***logos*** (word or discourse), this term is defined as the discourse or doctrine of the world.

Ecclesiology- The doctrine of the church; a term derived from ***ekklesia*** (church) and logos (word or discourse).

Ekklesia- the Greek term used by the New Testament writers to refer to the church. It was formerly used to refer to gatherings for political or business purposes.

Eschatology- From the Greek *escatos*, "the last, "last things," and *logos*, "the study of." In theology, eschatology is the study of the doctrine of future or last things. The doctrine of the last things. The terms refer to the end of history, embracing the Christian expectation of the return of Christ, the resurrection of the dead, the judgment of the living and dead, and the new heaven and new earth.

General Revelation- A term referring to any disclosure of God that does not rely upon the unrepeatable events of history.

Glossolalia- The Greek word for the speaking in tongues or the gifts of tongues.

Incarnation- From the Latin *in*, "in" and *caro*, "flesh." In theology, this is the doctrine that God, the Eternal Son—the second person of the Trinity—became man, or flesh, in the person of Jesus.

Justification- From the Hebrew *sadeq*, the Greek *dikaioo*, and the Latin *justificare*, "to justify," to pronounce, accept, and treat as just. In theology, it refers to God's pardoning sinners and restoring them to a state of righteousness.

Paul develops the doctrine of justification by faith in Romans and Galatians.

Kerygma- A Greek word meaning "that which is preached or proclaimed." In theology, the word was used to refer to the early Christian message of the gospel of Jesus Christ.

Kingdom of God (also synonymous with the kingdom of Heaven)- Refers to the reign of God through Jesus Christ in the lives of persons as evidenced by God's activity in, through, and around them.

Liberation Theology- A term used to refer to a group of theological movements such as third-world liberation movements, feminist theology, and black theology. Liberation theology views sin as man's inhumanity to man and not as rebellion. They emphasize deliverance from social, economic and political conditions, rather than reconciliation to God and the new birth.

Logos- The most common Greek term for "*word,*"and the source of the words **"*logic*"** and "wisdom." In ordinary Greek, logos means "*reason,*" though John used "Word" at the beginning of his gospel to refer to Jesus. John is saying that Jesus was and is God, the "Logic of God" or the "Wisdom of God" incarnate.

Messiah- The Hebrew *masiah*, the Aramaic *mesiha* or the Greek *christos* all mean "the anointed one." "Christ" is the Greek equivalent of the Hebrew "Messiah."

Ministry- From the Greek word diakoneo, "to serve," or douleuo, "to serve as a slave." In the New Testament, ministry is service to God and to other people in His name.

Monotheism- From the Greek *mono*, "one," and *theos*, "God." The Belief that there is one God and only one God.

Natural Theology- Knowledge about God that can be gained from the natural world— apart from special revelation—because the nature of creation reveals something of the nature of the Creator.

Ontological Argument- An argument for the existence of God put forward especially by the Inseam of Canterbury in his Proslogian (1079).

Ontology- From the Greek on, "***being***" and logos, "***logic,***" or "the study of." A doctrine of "being."

Paraclete- From the Greek ***parakletos,*** "one called to someone's aid." A theological term used to refer to the Person and work of the Holy Spirit. **Parakleteos** is often translated as "Comforter."

Parousia- The Greek word literally means "coming" or "arrival," and refers to the second coming of Christ. It includes the restoration of God's relationship to the individual, the corporate body of the church, the nation, and creation.

Pneumatology- From the Greek ***pneuma,*** "wind," "spirit," and *logos,* "the study of." Pneumatology, then, is the comprehensive study of the person, work, and doctrine of the Holy Spirit.

Redemption- A biblical term used in the understanding that God pays the price to restore human fellowship with Himself.

Revelation- From the Latin ***revelare,*** "to unveil," "to reveal."

Salvation- comes from the Greek word ***soterion,*** meaning to rescue, deliver, bring to safety, liberate, release, or cause preservation.

Sanctification- A doctrine of salvation expressing and emphasizing the aspect of growth and change in the Christian experience of God.

Soteriology- From the Greek ***soteria,*** "safety," and logos, "the study of." Soteriology is the branch of theology that studies salvation or the doctrine of salvation.

Special Revelation- The divine self-disclosure of God through unique and supernatural events.

Systematic Theology-The discipline that attempts to present, interpret, arrange, and justify in a consistent and meaningful way the teaching of Scripture. Systematic theology presents Scriptural truth in a coherent, understandable fashion to each age, relating Scripture to issues of practical Christian concerns.

Theocracy- From the Greek ***theokratia,*** from ***theos,*** "God," and ***kratein***, "to rule, to govern."

Theophany- A theological term for any visible or auditory manifestation of God. An encounter with God.

Vicarious Atonement- The Christian doctrine that Christ died in our place to pay the penalty for our sins.

ENDNOTES

1. Terry L. Miethe, *The Compact Dictionary of Doctrinal Words* (Minneapolis: Bethany House Publishers, 1988), p. 204.

2. John H. Sailhamer, *Christian Theology* (Grand Rapids: Zondervan Publishing House,1998), p. 12.

3. Ibid. 12.

4. A. J. Conyers, *A Basic Christian Theology* (Nashville: Broadman & Holman Publishers, 1995), p.5.

5. Sailhamer, p. 12.

6. Robert. A. Bennett, *God's Work of Liberation* (Wilton, Connecticut: Morehouse- Barlow Co., 1976), p.3.

7. Ibid. p. 37.

8. David S. Dockery, *Christian Scripture* (Nashville: Broadman & Holman Publishers, 1995), p.16.

9. David K. Beranrd, *Essential Doctrines of the Bible* (Hazelwood, MO: WORD AFLAME PRESS, 1988), p.4.

10. John H. Hayes & Carl R. Holladay, **Biblical Exegesis** (Atlanta: John Knox Press, 1982), p.5.

11. Dockery, p. 22.

12. Conyers, p. 4.

13. Owen C. Thomas, **Introduction To Theology** (Wilton, Connecticut: Morehouse-Barlow Co.Inc., 1983), p. 1.

14. Ibid. p. 1.

15. Ibid. p. 1.

16. Ibid. p. 2-4.

17. Conyers, p. 122.

18. Miethe, p. 192.

19. Roy T. Edgemon, **The Doctrines Baptist Believe** (Nashville: Convention Press, 1988), 76-77.

20. Ibid., p.111-112.

21. Miethe, p. 82.

22. Edgemon, p.126.

23. Miethe, p. 25.
24. Ibid., p. 25.

Selected Bibliography

Bernard, David K. **Essential Doctrines of the Bible**. Hazelwood, MD: WORD AFLAME PRESS, 1988.

Bickersteth, Edward H. **The Trinity**. Grand Rapids: Kregal Publications, 1957, 1996.

Carter, Mack King. **A Catechism For Baptist**. Winter Park, Florida: FOUR-G Publishers, Inc., 1996.

Conyers, A. J. **A Basic Christian Theology**. Nashville: Broadman & Holman Publishers, 1995.

Cottrell, Jack. **His Truths**. Joplin, Missouri: College Press Publishing Company, 1989.

Dockery, David S. **The Christian Scripture**. Nashville: Broadman & Holman Publishers, 1995.

Edgeman, Roy T. **The Doctrine Baptist Believe**. Nashville: Convention Press, 1998.

Evans, William. **The Great Doctrines of the Bible**. Chicago: Moody Press, 1974.

Gibbs, Alfred P. and others. **What Christians Believe**. Chicago: Emmaus Bible School, 1951.

Harris, James H. **Pastoral Theology "A Black Perspective."** Minneapolis: Fortress Press, 1991.

Hayes, John H. & Carl R. Holladay. *Biblical Exegesis*. Atlanta: John Knox Press, 1982.

Little, Paul E. *Know What You Believe*. Colorado Springs: Chariot Victor Publishing, 1999.

Lutzer, Erwin. *The Doctrines That Divide.* Grand Rapids: Kregel Publications, 1998.

Miethe, Terry L. *The Compact Dictionary of Doctrinal Words*. Minneapolis: Bethany House Publishers, 1988.

Robinson, Darrell W. *The Doctrine of Salvation*. Nashville: Convention Press, 1992.

Ryrie, Charles C. *A Survey of Bible Doctrine*. Chicago: Moody Press, 1972.

Ryrie, Charles C. *Biblical Theology of the New Testament*. Chicago: Moody Press, 1987.

Sailhamer, John H. *Christian Theology*. Grand Rapids: Zondervan Publishing House, 1998.

Wilmore, Gayraud S. and Cone, James H. *Black Theology: A Documentary History, 1966-1979*. New York: Orbis Books, 1979.

Zuck, Roy B., Editor. *A Biblical Theology of the New Testament*. Chicago: Moody Bible Press, 1994.

Contact Information

If you would like to correspond with Dr. Benjamin Hinton in response to this book, or schedule a speaking engagement, you may contact him at: hinton@chosenwordpublishing.com .

You will also find more contact information at www.eteamministry.org.

**CHECK OUT CHOSEN WORD PUBLISHING'S
BOOKS ONLINE AT:
www.chosenwordpublishing.com**